From Inside

Ezra MacKay

Presentation by *BookLeaf Publishing*

Web: www.bookleafpub.com

E-mail: info@bookleafpub.com

ISBN: 978-93-95784-64-1

First edition 2022

*This is dedicated to anyone who has felt unseen,
unheard, weird, strange, alone, a stranger in
their own body or unknown.*

Always questioning.

You are my people!

ACKNOWLEDGEMENT

Well what can I say I am in shock this is actually happening!
This publication of my poems was solely to fulfill a personal dream of mine that just happened to come true because of a random opportunity. Because of this I also only told a handful of people that I was even going to publish my poems.
I don't have many people to thank this time but I would like to thank Bookleaf Publishing for believing anyone should be able to have the random opportunity to publish, to finally realize a dream of mine that I had always thought would never happen.

I will also thank my partner Void who has literally been by my side in different capacities since high school. They supported me in any way they could through most of these experiences that inspired me to write about it.
So in a way, they have been a part of each of my poems since the beginning.

Void, I love you with the power of infinite kitty purrs and will love you until the end of all times in all dimensions in all of the universes across all the galaxies past, present and future.

PREFACE

Since I was a teenager I have written poems on and off. Sometimes based on an experience I've had, some just an idea, words that needed to flow to paper.
These poems are my thoughts, feelings and emotions right on paper. I am scared to have other people read them but I am super excited to share them with you.

This first volume of poems I've titled "Teen Edition" because it is just exactly that. These poems are from the period of high school to young adult and deals with all kinds is thoughts and emotions I was going through during that period in my life such as self harm and suicide.

Mental health has become very important to me and sharing experiences about what it's like, what it feels like living with mental illnesses etc. - I don't know if you will relate to any of the feelings that come through my writing but if you do, know that you are not alone.

Scratches

the scratches are like stones
they are always there,
solid and free.

the blade is like a smooth caress
inflicting but contradicting,
painful and escaping.

the pain is like freedom
it comes with a price,
the blood and scars.

the blood is like pride
you have to lose some before you understand,
shed tears and gained freedom.

A smile

A smile may look nice
may stop tears
may heal a hurt
but a smile never cost a cent.

A smile may be fake
may cause more hurt
may create more understanding
but a smile never loses touch.

A smile may create a presence
may touch a soul
may shatter a silence
but a smile never kills a dream, a hope, a life.

Priceless

Now feelings mean nothing,
I can't believe it's true,
But saying I don't care,
That would be a lie.

Thinking about the other day,
And how they stopped to laugh,
It's something I never wanted to happen,
But I don't usually get my way.

Whenever I see them,
My chest starts to hurt,
Salty little tears fill my eyes,
As they laugh the tears fall and my feet run.

When they look at me,
They smile like they have a secret,
As they look right through me,
Acting like I'm not even there.

Writing notes in class,
Passing them back on break,
Telling each other secrets,
That was the meaning of fun.

But one time she wrote a note,
It told me our friendship was done,
I stared at it and cried,
Oh how I hated that note.

I decided to write her back,
She was so shocked,
She didn't even want us to be best friends,
All along I thought we were.

I would cry myself to sleep,
Nights on end confused,
Thinking I lost 2 of my best friends,
Until my true best friend told me I was too good.

The only thing I want to remember,
The day I told her I didn't need her,
The look on that backstabbers face,
That was truly priceless.

Hide

hello incense burning
the scent terrifies me
the sight betrays me
he beckons to me
i walk into the room
the children look away
the candles go out
i look around but im alone
the scene vanishes as in a play
im standing in a little cafe in Italy
again he beckons to me
i look away as his eyes burn into mine
the chiming of the clock betrays the silence
i open my eyes yet again and im not there
im not there
im floating somewhere high above him
but i dont know why
i chance a look down and fall
i seem to fall forever
til i hit the earth
but he is there to pick me up
to save me from myself
i thank him but suddenly
he turns into the me i tried to run from
im being beckoned to reembrace

to become again what i tried to hide
i tried to hide from it
i tried to hide it deep inside
but it escaped from me
raging and burning
i accept my fate
we become one again

Men, you should know

When you see us walking
in 2's + 3's whispering
over coffee we are

talking about you

how you disappear
into the dawn + ride
off into the sunset
with our hearts

how you enter us
out of the blue + leave
in pink + purples

how we long to lie
beside you
telling truths + how we
long to make love
without falling
into it

how we know you
hurt too wanting to
channel it away take it

on ourselves + make
everything better how
it pains us
not to be able to

touch you.

On your knees

How can you be so cruel
to push me away
to leave me standing there
but to not leave
just to see me fall
then you laugh
and walk away
but don't worry
I can pick myself up
handle this mess
start over better
make you jealous
make you come running back
to me, yeah, me
but I'll just look at you
then laugh
and walk away
I'll look back
and see you fall
to your knees
just like you did to me
so I left you there
on your knees

Sweet gift

to kill me now would be such a sweet gift
but somehow you just can't pull the trigger
i said i loved you no matter what happened
but you still seemed to think i was lying
i'm standing here crying in disbelief
screaming "i don't understand"
but you continue to give me that look
and you say that i know what you mean
now i give up i can't do this anymore
i'm taking my bag and i'm taking my stuff
i'm leaving you now i won't look back
i can't stand here and do this again
we've gone through this over and over
i'm in so much pain but you don't see it
i need to stop this i'm going in circles
i though for sure we'd be married by now
but the time never seemed to come around
now the time has come for me to leave
i'm bored and i need to move on
you won't let me but i'm going to anyways
it's killing me to see you standing there waiting
as i take my things and walk out the door
so to kill me now would be such a sweet gift

Sanity

all eyes on me
all alone, i stumble
and fall
i throw my arms out to brace myself
and i fall into nothingness, again
tears welling up in my eyes
i look for you in the crowd
i'm not surprised as i don't find you
you're never there
you never thought to ask
about something that means so much to me
and yet so little to you
i turn away slowly smiling to myself
thinking to myself
"they must think i'm insane"
but i realized
this is where i belong
in the midst of sanity
completely insane and alone

Tell me

Tell me when
When
Does it get better
When
Does the pain stop
When
Do I begin to feel again
Feel anything
The sun on my face
The wind in my hair
The way you touch my hand
But all I can feel
Is the way you pull away
The way my heart shatters
Spilling out over everything

The feeling slipping away
Have I forgotten already
What it was like before
Before you, before this
Is this all I am?
Tell me

Love

love is a tidal wave emotion
taking over your entire being

love is the randomest of thoughts
making you smile in the dark

love is like the face of a child
all smiles and glowing

love is a child's laughter
ringing clear with joy

love is the tears on your face
the night after your first heartbreak

love is the smile on your face
when their name shows up on caller ID

love is the peek out the window
every 5 seconds after they say "on the way"

love is the racing of your heart
when you hear the expected knock on the door

love is the gentlest of touches
when they take your hand and say "I do."

beautiful relief

the pain drives through my arm
the blood rushes like a raging river
my face is frozen in time
that second where i seem the vanish
and everything is so perfect
then people bring me back to reality
i am unmoved by their concern
i realize i'm not at home
but still in class
and that was all in my head
but i run for that place again
my music screaming in my ears
and i sigh frozen in place
my mind throws me into a wave of relief
i suddenly feel like i'm moving
jerked back into reality i realize i am
without even noticing
i've walked to my next class
walking through the halls
like a beautiful zombie
(emphasis on zombie)
people think this is something you do all your
life
or its just a phase we go through

for me it's a state of the mind
this beautiful relief of mine

To a Stranger

This is a letter to a stranger
who's not quite a complete stranger
we've talked but never met
so where does that leave us
as friends or foes?

You seem to really like me
but i know nothing about you
my head and heart seem torn in two
this is leaving me asking
so do i like you too?

You want to ask me
you say pick a ring
i know how you feel
but i'm so young and confused
could you give me a minute to think?

You're moving this so fast
i'm not sure i understand
i haven't had time to listen to my heart
this would be why i'm writing this
this letter to a stranger.

Why

Why should I give up my life
Why should I give up my innocence
just because he wants me to
has he ever thought of what I want
does it even mean anything to him
does he care about my opinion
does he care about my feelings
because I'm getting a feeling he doesn't
I can't be certain I'm doing the right thing
it feels so right but I still don't know
people keep telling me different things
but my mind just wants one answer
is he for real to me forever
can I trust him maybe love him
people say their minds get stuck
for me it's my heart that's stuck
tell me please is he good enough

The evil

Hiding in the darkness
running from the light
the evil still lives inside
No matter how much you deny it
What secrets are you hiding
behind that mask of nonconformity
Trusting no one not even yourself
Where's the sunshine on your rainy day
forever an emotionless victim of life
The evil is now raging within
I can see it every time I look in your eyes
I can see it past the darkness
You can no longer hide behind
your mask of perfect frailty
It has been shattered and broken
You like to think you're in control
of the evil threatening to take over
But the truth is your life isn't yours
and your soul is gone forever
Eaten away at by the evil
The evil you have now become

love peak

spinning round and round
you smile like nothings wrong
but i know the truth
its all over and you dont care
you push me away and lie
i wanna scream i wanna cry
i wanna break down in tears
just to show the world how much i really care
the people keep on smiling
even though they are gone
the love peak just burns
a memory once forgotten
turns to ashes in my hands
you blow it away and tell me to go home
like you never realized how much i really care
you cant see me anymore behind the lies
the clock keeps ticking
seconds passing away like dead flowers
i let it get infected by you
i have no power over healing
i tried to ignore the way you made me feel
i took so many painkillers
just to make it numb
but its so hard
when you were all i wanted

Portrait of Innocence

There you sit quietly
all dressed in white
Picking at your fingernails
Biting your lip until it bleeds
You're just like a child
Innocent until proven guilty
by an all knowing parent
Naïve to the world around you
it's such a Kodak moment to see
when you finally wipe the sadness from you and
smile
the whole room seems brighter than it once was
What a portrait of innocence
You look just like a porcelain doll
hand painted and ready to break
at the second something goes wrong
You're always bracing yourself for the fall
but the push never comes to destroy you
so it leaves you standing there holding yourself
together
although you have not yet fallen apart or broken
It looks so sweet when you walk over and hold
onto him
knowing he'll protect you from everything
and then your life seems to balance out

Now everything seems so perfect to you
What a portrait of innocence

A life perceived

Broken windows and tangled hearts,
birds in flight,
everything's in motion.

Life running too fast,
feels like you're in reverse,
can't keep a straight face.

Sunbeams falling from the sky,
dying trees,
people go out dancing.

Going through life with no feeling,
bored out of your mind,
end up with more work than you started with.

See new people,
go to new places,
never the same way twice.

Fashion magazines,
designed for the celebrities,
have no effect on our society.

People having early deaths,
all caused by too much stress,
rushing all over the place.

Never enough time,
and always too much work,
no wonder people go crazy.

Two paths

There are two paths before you
which one you will chose you don't know
but then again you do know
You're forever stuck in the middle
never truly going one way or the other
but somehow seeming quite content
Both ways seem interesting enough
but you don't care you're good where you are
Most people think you're confused
or that there's something wrong with you
But you know in your heart where you're going
people just don't approve or think much of it
Sometimes I think you're luckier than the rest
because you get the best of both worlds
and I can see you love it no matter what
I can see you smiling like there's nothing to it
and you know what you're doing
Walking and talking without a care
Now you see the two paths before you
and they've become just one

Smile

tears that fall down like rain
they hit the pillow like gunshots
and draw tracks down my cheeks.
as i lay in bed and hear the whirl of the fan
thinking it may be all the thoughts running
through my mind.
looking up i see lights flashing across my ceiling
out the window i see a train passing by,
wishing i could be standing there on the tracks
never looking back.
my hands clench into fists as i recall the last
words
you said to me before you left, "i just dont feel
it."
i sob and turn my head towards the wall
looking for something to stop my mind from
numbing
i see the blood slowly trickling down from my
fist.
i lay there confused for a moment until i feel the
pain
looking down at my hands i realize what ive
done.
as i drift away on a silver cloud i smile,
and paint the world red with my blood.

Am I crazy?

am i crazy?
just because i live alone
talk to myself
and have invisible friends?

am i crazy?
just because you see me wandering alone
never very sociable
and always seem to know the answer?

am i crazy?
just because i have weird habits
do things most people wouldnt
and never seem to smile?

am i crazy?
just because i seem to understand everyone's
problems
but never have an answer
and really like cats?

you must be the crazy one
because you cant seem to stop judging me
are always scared, running away from me
and never seem to leave me alone.
am i really the crazy one?

I'll always remember

I'll always remember
those late walks
finally leaving the school grounds at 6
the hot tub parties that meant nothing
and the talks at midnight that meant everything

I'll always remember
grape crush and us is a lethal combination
the times we had characters was more fun than
I'll ever know
all the school assemblies we attended
but never what was said in them

I'll always remember
each day was as different as the next
each weekend the same, sleepovers
my high school years were the best years
each day tattooed perfectly in my mind

I'll always remember
every inside joke and every story
every wild trip to mcdonalds
every giggle and whisper over guys
all the time spent on the phone without a word
being said

I'll always remember
the late nights and early sunrises
every ridiculous text sent and received
all the random gifts exchanged
every single lunch hour spent playing video
games

I'll always remember
because
I'll never forget.